I Love My Pet
SALAMANDER

Aaron Carr

Go to **www.av2books.com**, and enter this book's unique code.

BOOK CODE

A439958

AV² by Weigl brings you media enhanced books that support active learning.

AV² provides enriched content that supplements and complements this book. Weigl's AV² books strive to create inspired learning and engage young minds in a total learning experience.

Your AV² Media Enhanced books come alive with...

Audio
Listen to sections of the book read aloud.

Video
Watch informative video clips.

Embedded Weblinks
Gain additional information for research.

Try This!
Complete activities and hands-on experiments.

Key Words
Study vocabulary, and complete a matching word activity.

Quizzes
Test your knowledge.

Slide Show
View images and captions, and prepare a presentation.

... and much, much more!

Published by AV² by Weigl
350 5th Avenue, 59th Floor   New York, NY   10118
Websites: www.av2books.com   www.weigl.com

Library of Congress Cataloging-in-Publication Data

Carr, Aaron.
 Salamander / Aaron Carr.
    pages cm. -- (I love my pet)
 ISBN 978-1-4896-3106-0 (hardcover : alk. paper) -- ISBN 978-1-4896-3107-7 (softcover : alk. paper) -- ISBN 978-1-4896-3108-4 (single-user ebk.) -- ISBN 978-1-4896-3109-1 (multi-user ebk.)
 1. Salamanders--Juvenile literature. 2. Salamanders as pets--Juvenile literature. I. Title.
 QL668.C2C37 2014
 639.3'785--dc23
                              2014038598

Printed in the United States of America in North Mankato, Minnesota
1 2 3 4 5 6 7 8 9 0 18 17 16 15 14

112014
WEP311214

Project Coordinator: Katie Gillespie   Art Director: Terry Paulhus

Weigl acknowledges Getty Images and iStock as the primary image suppliers for this title.

I Love My Pet
SALAMANDER

CONTENTS

I love my pet salamander.
I take good care of her.

5

My pet salamander was born under water.
She looked like a small fish.

8

My pet salamander lived under water for about three months. She grew legs at this time.

Some salamanders live in the water for years.

My pet salamander
has smooth skin.
Her skin is covered
in slime.

My pet salamander has a long tail. She uses her tail to help her swim.

A salamander can drop its tail and grow it back later.

13

My pet salamander lives in a large tank. I clean her tank once a week.

My pet salamander likes to hide. I make sure I do not bother her.

Most salamanders sleep during the day and stay awake at night.

My pet salamander eats bugs.
I feed her at night.

19

20

I make sure my pet salamander is healthy and happy.
I love my pet salamander.

SALAMANDER FACTS

These pages provide more detail about the interesting facts found in the book. They are intended to be used by adults as a learning support to help young readers round out their knowledge of each animal featured in the *I Love My Pet* series.

Pages 4–5

I love my pet salamander. I take good care of her. Salamanders are amphibians. They are related to frogs and toads. There are more than 400 species of salamanders. Salamanders do not need to be bathed, groomed, or walked. This makes them easier to care for than many other types of pets. However, having a salamander as a pet is still an important responsibility.

Pages 6–7

My pet salamander was born under water. She looked like a small fish. Different species of salamanders go through varying life cycles. Many of these life cycles have four stages. First, salamanders hatch from eggs. The eggs are laid in a group, called a clutch. After hatching, the salamander is usually in the larval stage. The larva has feathery gills on the sides of its head. This helps it breathe under water.

Pages 8–9

My pet salamander lived under water for about three months. She grew legs at this time. The next stage of salamander development is metamorphosis. During this third stage, the fishlike larva grows legs, eyelids, a tongue, and lungs, and loses its external gills. Salamanders reach maturity in the final stage. Some species live on land, some live in the water, and others live both on land and in water.

Pages 10–11

My pet salamander has smooth skin. Her skin is covered in slime. Unlike reptiles, salamanders do not have scales. They have soft skin. Glands in the salamander's skin make a thick layer of slime. This covers the skin and keeps it from becoming too dry. The slime of brightly colored salamanders may also be poisonous.

Pages 12–13

My pet salamander has a long tail. She uses her tail to help her swim. Salamanders are the only amphibians that have a tail as an adult. They use their tails to propel themselves through the water when swimming. Their tails also provide better balance and maneuverability on land. Salamanders can drop their tails if caught by predators.

Pages 14–15

My pet salamander lives in a large tank. I clean her tank once a week. Most salamanders need a 10 gallon (38 liter) aquarium or terrarium. The enclosure should include both land and water areas. There should be a lid to keep the air inside warm and humid. Salamanders also need plants, rocks, and other objects to hide behind.

Pages 16–17

My pet salamander likes to hide. I make sure I do not bother her. Most salamanders are nocturnal. They spend part of the day hiding. They may dig into soil or hide under leaves, rocks, or logs. Salamanders are usually active at night. They should be kept in a dark, quiet place where they will not be afraid to move around at night.

Pages 18–19

My pet salamander eats bugs. I feed her at night. Salamanders are carnivores, or meat-eaters. They eat insects, worms, tadpoles, shrimp, and small fish. Salamanders prefer live food, but they will sometimes eat frozen food that has been thawed. Depending on the species, salamanders may eat underwater or on land. Young salamanders must be fed every day. Mature salamanders only eat every two or three days.

Pages 20–21

I make sure my pet salamander is healthy and happy. I love my pet salamander. Salamanders need food, fresh water, a clean enclosure, and a safe place to hide. They like to be left alone. Handling a salamander causes it stress and may lead to bites. When bringing a salamander home, give it time to adjust to its new surroundings.

KEY WORDS

Research has shown that as much as 65 percent of all written material published in English is made up of 300 words. These 300 words cannot be taught using pictures or learned by sounding them out. They must be recognized by sight. This book contains 46 common sight words to help young readers improve their reading fluency and comprehension. This book also teaches young readers several important content words, such as proper nouns. These words are paired with pictures to aid in learning and improve understanding.

Page	Sight Words First Appearance
4	good, her, I, my, of, take
6	a, like, she, small, under, was, water
9	about, at, for, in, live, some, the, this, three, time, years
11	has, is
12	and, back, can, grow, help, it, its, later, long, to, uses
15	large, once
16	day, do, make, most, night, not
18	eats

Page	Content Words First Appearance
4	care, pet, salamander
6	fish
9	legs, months
11	skin, slime
12	tail
15	tank, week
16	bugs